DISCARDED

Aboriginal Legends of Canada

Algonquin

Megan Cuthbert

Weigl

Published by Weigl Educational Publishers Limited
6325 10th Street SE
Calgary, Alberta T2H 2Z9
Website: www.weigl.ca

Library and Archives Canada Cataloguing in Publication
Cuthbert, Megan, 1984-, author
       Algonquin / Megan Cuthbert.
(Aboriginal legends of Canada)
Issued in print and electronic formats.
ISBN 978-1-77071-295-9 (bound).--ISBN 978-1-77071-296-6 (pbk.).--
ISBN 978-1-77071-297-3 (ebook)

       1. Algonquin Indians--Folklore. I. Title.

E99.A349C88 2013   j398.2089'9733   C2013-907320-5
                                                 C2013-907321-3

Printed in the United States of America in North Mankato, Minnesota
1 2 3 4 5 6 7 8 9 0 18 17 16 15 14

062014
WEP301113

Editor: Heather Kissock
Design: Mandy Christiansen
Illustrator: Martha Jablonski-Jones

Photo Credits
Weigl acknowledges Getty Images and Alamy as its primary image suppliers for this title.

We acknowledge the financial support of the Government of Canada through the Canada Book Fund for our publishing activities.

CONTENTS

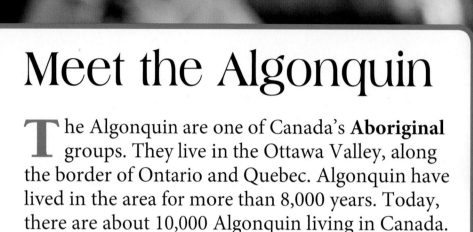

Meet the Algonquin

The Algonquin are one of Canada's **Aboriginal** groups. They live in the Ottawa Valley, along the border of Ontario and Quebec. Algonquin have lived in the area for more than 8,000 years. Today, there are about 10,000 Algonquin living in Canada. Most live on **reserves** in Quebec and Ontario.

Storytelling has long been a part of Algonquin life. Even today, storytellers visit schools to pass along stories and **legends** from long ago. Telling stories helps the Algonquin share their **culture** with younger generations.

Stories of Creation

Stories help connect the Algonquin to their history and to each other. One of the most important stories the Algonquin tell is the story of creation. This story explains how the Algonquin believe the world and its creatures came to be.

Nanabozho is just one of several characters found in Algonquin stories. Glooscap is a heroic figure. Nokomis is a grandmother figure who brings the riches of the earth to the Algonquin people. Widjigo is an evil spirit.

Many Algonquin stories feature a character named Nanabozho. Nanabozho is known for both his wisdom and mischievous nature. *Nanabozho's Flood* tells how Nanabozho used his wisdom to help his animal friends after a great flood destroyed the land.

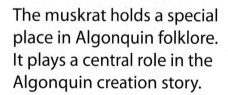

The muskrat holds a special place in Algonquin folklore. It plays a central role in the Algonquin creation story.

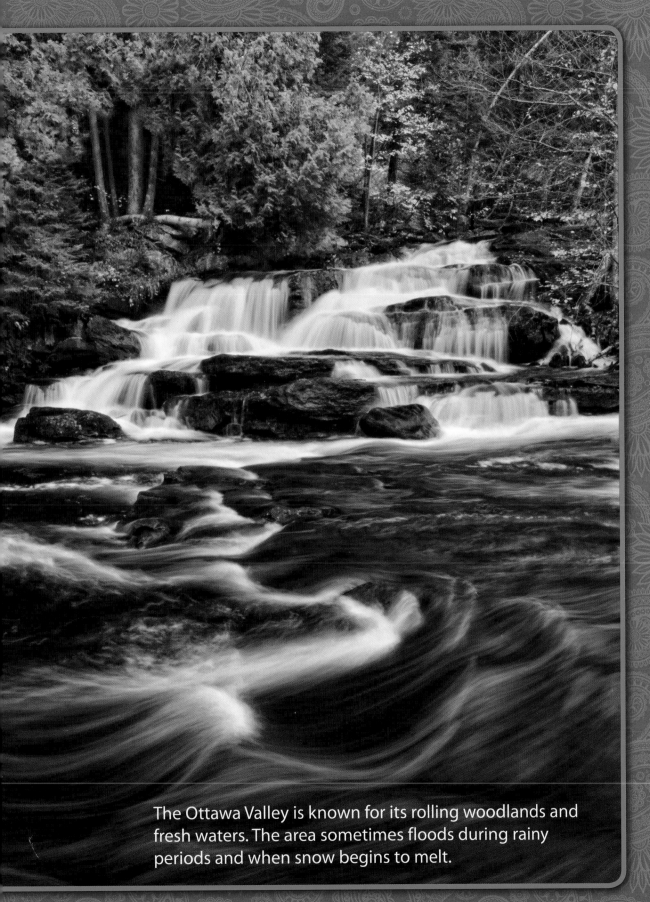

The Ottawa Valley is known for its rolling woodlands and fresh waters. The area sometimes floods during rainy periods and when snow begins to melt.

Nanabozho's FLOOD

One day, Nanabozho was relaxing along the bank of a river when he noticed the water beginning to rise. To avoid getting wet, he began to back away from it. Soon, he found himself on top of a mountain.

The water continued to rise. Nanabozho knew that it would not be long before the water would catch up to him. He had to find somewhere else to go and a way to get there. He quickly grabbed two logs and made a raft.

As he rode the water's current, Nanabozho saw many of his animal friends. They were upset because they thought they might drown in the flood. Nanabozho asked them to find him some soil. Only the muskrat responded, bringing Nanabozho a small pile of soil.

Nanabozho looked down at the soil and gently blew on it. The soil spread out and grew, creating the land on which we now live.

Nature Stories

In the past, the Algonquin relied on nature to provide for their needs. As **hunter-gatherers**, they used the plants and animals around them for food. They also used the skin and bones from the animals to make clothing and tools.

Many stories tell of the important role animals played in Algonquin life. Some stories explain an animal's behaviour. Others describe why animals look the way they do. *The Colours of the Sunset* explains how the pollywog, or tadpole, came to have gills.

A pollywog is a frog or toad that is not fully grown.

Moose was a staple meat for the Algonquin. The animal's antlers and bones were used to make snares, knives, and other tools.

The COLOURS of the SUNSET

There once was a boy who was very good-natured and never gave his parents any trouble. However, every day at sunset he would start crying and could not be stopped. Medicine Woman explained that the boy craved the colours of the sunset. She said the only place to find them was at the bottom of a large lake.

The boy's father went to the lake, but it was guarded by an enormous pollywog. The man caught the pollywog and glued its mouth shut so the other fish would not hear its cries for help. The man then dove deep into the lake to look for the colours of the sunset. When he found them, he took the colours back to his son.

The other fish were angry at the pollywog for not guarding the lake. As punishment, they created gills and made the pollywog breathe through them. Ever since, all pollywogs are born with small puckered mouths and gills.

Life Lessons

Algonquin parents and **elders** use stories to teach important lessons to their children. Many Algonquin stories teach children about behaving properly. They show what can happen when people misbehave. These stories have a serious message, but include funny elements. Children enjoy the humour of the story while still learning a lesson.

Everyone in an Algonquin community had a role to play. Men hunted and protected the group from harm. Women cooked, made clothes, and cared for children. Children helped the adults with their work.

Rabbit Calls a Truce tells the story of Rabbit and Otter. The two friends like to tease and play tricks on each other. When their friends are in trouble, however, the two team up to help. The story teaches children a lesson about teamwork. Working together is an important part of Algonquin life.

Nanabozho is often portrayed as a rabbit in Algonquin stories.

The Algonquin made decisions as a group. The men and women of a community would meet to discuss problems and search for solutions together.

RABBIT Calls a TRUCE

Otter and Rabbit were always playing tricks on each other. One day, Otter was chasing Rabbit when the two came to a town of starving people. Someone had been stealing their food. Rabbit thumped his hind leg and said to Otter, "We must find the robbers and punish them!" Otter quickly agreed.

The two began working together to find the robbers. They soon discovered that a group of weasels and mice were stealing from the people. Otter and Rabbit pretended to join them in their plan. However, on their way to town, the two tricked the other animals and led them off a cliff. The weasels and mice fell into the sea.

After saving the people from starvation, Rabbit and Otter continued to chase and play tricks on each other. Despite their mischief, the two friends had no greed or spite in their hearts.

Heroic Tales

Many Algonquin legends feature characters that make great effort to help others. These heroes possess the **traits** the Algonquin most admire. They are known for being brave, smart, and kind.

Glooscap is often portrayed as a teacher and caretaker of the Algonquin people. *How Glooscap Found the Summer* describes the long journey Glooscap took to save his people from the cold. In the story, Glooscap must outsmart Winter. He must be persistent in his journey and use his wits and charm to bring balance to the world.

Summer was a time to gather food for winter. Meat was often combined with berries and dried to make *pimikan*. This provided the Algonquin with food when animals were hard to find.

Winter could be difficult for the Algonquin. Waters were frozen, so they could not use canoes to travel. Most winter travel was done on foot using snowshoes.

How GLOOSCAP Found the SUMMER

Glooscap was a good leader to his people. One day, it grew extremely cold, and snow covered the land. People began dying from cold and hunger. Winter had frozen the land. Glooscap went north to talk with Winter about the problem. Winter did not want to talk. Instead, he cast a spell on Glooscap, making Glooscap fall asleep for six months.

When Glooscap awoke, he went south to see if Summer would help save his people from the cold. He travelled a long time before he found Summer in the middle of a forest. He convinced Summer to come back north with him and talk to Winter. Together, Glooscap and Summer managed to charm Winter. Slowly, the ice and snow melted away. Summer and Winter made an agreement that, for six months of the year, Winter would reign over Glooscap's land. Then, Summer would return from the south and bring warmer weather for the next six months.

Activity

Make a Moose Caller

The moose was one of the animals the Algonquin hunted for food. When hunting, the Algonquin would use a moose caller to bring the animal to them. Follow these instructions to create your own moose caller.

You will need:

Tape

Bristol board

Scissors

Ruler

1. With an adult's help, cut the bristol board into a square about 30.5 centimeters in diameter.

2. Roll the square from one corner to another, making a cone. Tape the seam together to hold the cone in shape.

3. Fold the pieces at the wide end into the cone. Tape them so that the wide end is even all the way around.

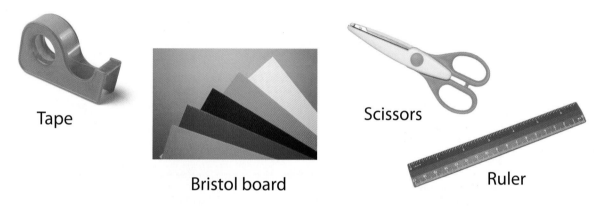

4. Blow into the cone to see if you can make a sound.

Further Research

Many books and websites provide information on Aboriginal legends. To learn more about this topic, borrow books from the library, or search the internet.

Books

Most libraries have computers that connect to a database for researching information. If you input a key word, you will be provided with a list of books in the library that contain information on that topic. Nonfiction books are arranged numerically, using their call number. Fiction books are organized alphabetically by the author's last name.

Websites

Learn more about the Algonquin at: www. anishinabenation.ca/eng/alg_history_en.htm

To read more Algonquin legends, visit: www.native-languages.org/algonquin-legends.htm

Key Words

Aboriginal: First Nations, Inuit, and Métis of Canada

culture: the arts, beliefs, and habits of a community, people, or country

elders: the wise people of a community

hunter-gatherers: people who hunt animals and look for plants instead of growing crops and raising livestock

legends: stories that have been passed down from generation to generation

reserves: land set aside for First Nations to live on

traits: qualities or characteristics

Index